Business Conflict Resolution

B. Vincent

Published by RWG Publishing, 2021.

BUSINESS CONFLICT RESOLUTION

First edition. June 21, 2021.

Written by B. Vincent.

Also by B. Vincent

Affiliate Marketing
Affiliate Marketing
Affiliate Marketing

Standalone
Affiliate Recruiting
Business Layoffs & Firings
Business and Entrepreneur Guide
Business Remote Workforce
Career Transition
Project Management
Precision Targeting
Professional Development
Strategic Planning
Content Marketing
Imminent List Building
Getting Past GateKeepers
Banner Ads
Bookkeeping
Bridge Pages
Business Acquisition
Business Bogging

Marketing Automation
Better Meetings
Business Conflict Resolution

Business Conflict Resolution

unde and Flanagan once said the better able team members are to
engage, speak, listen, hear, interpret and respond constructively, the
re likely their teams are to leverage conflict rather than be leveled by
And Dale Carnegie reminds us when dealing with people, remember,
're not dealing with creatures of logic, but creatures of emotion.
adling conflicts in the workplace can be an intimidating and
ttractive prospect. But handling them badly or not handling them at
s sure to make things even worse. Conflicts, whether they involve you
whether they're among other members of your team can seriously
aage your organization's climate if not dealt with right away. But how
we properly resolve conflicts and disputes in a way that minimizes
atisfaction from both parties and positively impacts our
anization? In this course, we're going to teach you how to do exactly
t.

85% of employees go through conflicts which disrupt work and
vents smooth collaboration. 24% of a manager's day is spent handling
flict, though this doesn't mean that this time is spent positively
aedying it. Conflict can create tension and recent statistics show that
% of employees resign due to a company's toxic office environment.
ase statistics show that conflict resolution is an increasingly important
a that businesses should focus on. Our course is going to consist of a
es of critical discussion points. These are designed to cover this broad
ic as thoroughly as possible, to encourage growth in these vital areas,
l to facilitate a real and fruitful discussion within your organization
ut how you can each improve on this essential characteristic both

at work and in your personal lives in general. Some of these wil
pretty lengthy, and some will be relatively straightforward and b
At the very end of this roadmap comes the most important final s
discussion time. Do not skip this. This is the most important par
this training. When you finish this course, you need to spend at l
an hour or so going over the questions we supply at the end as a gr
Whoever's the head honcho in the group should designate a facilit
whose responsibility it is that each question is covered, and that every
time permitting, is able to have their say. Make sure that all contributi
are valued, all suggestions considered, and all opinions respected. So,
move into the first discussion point.

No matter who you are, conflict is always bound to happen. Whe
you're a manager or a staff member, there's always going to be con
in the workplace. Conflicts are normal, healthy even, but they can ca
everything to come to a screeching halt. Your workflow, y
productivity. One can't avoid conflict, because negative emotions
up and create a toxic work environment. Allow conflicts to sit too l
and they become a liability to the company. For everyone's sake, hi
manager or supervisor who isn't afraid of dealing with drama. Deal v
the issue as soon as you can. It's wonderful to work out the conflict
moment you realize it's there. But a word of advice, try giving the par
a bit of time to collect themselves before the talk. If they seem to be v
heated about the conflict, it's better to let the parties sleep on it and
it out the following day. Having everyone be level headed and compo
going into the meeting will make conflict resolution considerably ea
Sort out your feelings before you get started. Calmly helping two par
who are antagonizing one another to solve a problem may se
daunting, but think of it as an opportunity. There wouldn't be
conflict if there were no problems at all with how you're running
company. Before you have the talking to with the parties dire
involved, you can suggest that they name each emotion they feel at
time. They then have to ask themselves the question, why do I feel

s? It'll help them get a clearer picture of the whole dispute and make discussion smoother. Have a talk, person to person. Meet the parties e to face in a private space. And for an adequate period of time. ery one directly involves has to be in the same room to resolve the ie. Make sure that the meeting isn't too soon, nor too late ie terms of ximity from the incident, as well as the time of day. Do be careful as some people being asked to a meeting with your boss and the person 1 have a problem with can feel intimidating. This may feed into the gative emotions that were already present due to the conflict. You can id this by clearly defining the meetings details, the time, the venue, at the meeting is about, and if possible, its goals.

Having a private meeting with your employees to work through conflict will help quell rumors. If there are already existing rumors, audible 06:42] quell them as soon as possible. Speak in a professional nner. There should be an atmosphere of professionalism, peace and ety in the room to facilitate a smooth discussion. If one party gets too ruptive during the discussion, you remind everyone that it isn't for u, though, it'll definitely help the company a lot, best not to add this t loud. The main goal is for your employees to find closure. Here are ys to use respectful communication. Use objective neutral language, can help avoid escalation as well as avoid alienating the other party. oid name calling, insults and the like. This will keep the opposing side m feeling that they are being belittled or attacked. It also goes without ing that course violent language should also be avoided. Cursing is solutely reprehensible and must be stifled immediately. Be fair to eryone involved. The parties talking to each other first can eliminate e need for an intervention. However, if they don't speak to one other, or they have to talk and come to an agreement, or don't talk and imediately move to starting a commotion at work, it'll be paramount r a third party to step in. There may be a chance that you, the third rty have made friends with one or more people involved. It's not cessary to renounce your friendship with them. But you still need to

be fair and impartial when handling the conflict. Take care not to m
with the parties one by one, there's a chance that you'll have two sto
that do not quite match up, as both sides will want to be in the right e
if they don't mean to. It would be best to speak to everyone all toget
from the beginning.

Make use of the rule book. It's best to outline the compar
preexisting rules and regulations early on. All the better if it's got ru
dealing with conflict in particular, define how your organization sol
issues, and there'll be less chances of staff causing conflict and even l
of any confusion when one arises. Try to go over the company rulebo
or policies. See if you have a section on handling conflict if not a mod
that's detailed, clear, and uncontestable. If the regulations aren't cl
enough, it's imperative to read through them or at least an abridg
version of them before starting to solve the matter at hand. Once you
got that down, you can direct your attention to the employees. Keep
mind that emotions which are natural for people to experience are val
but behavior will be subject to scrutiny. Be forgiving. Your employ
may be subconsciously thinking they'll be punished for havi
arguments or disagreements that disrupted the usual work day. T
might add unwarranted stress to the encounter, and cause them to
in a way that you believe they're the one on the right. Assure them tl
this isn't a fight to see who's right and who's wrong, you should let th
know at the outset, that they aren't in danger of getting any sort
penalty, much less being dismissed from their job. This will allow fo
less self-centered discussion. If you're one of the parties embroiled in t
conflict, be prepared to apologize. Your fault may not even be somethi
that you realized you did. But regardless, you need to apologize. A
when you do, it should come from the heart.

Direct and guide the discussion, if you're the neutral party, handli
the conflict, be even handed all the way to the end. This goes doul
for managers. You're the leader of the pack, the team looks to you
solve the issue at hand and put it to rest. To help you out, here's t

IR method. It guides the way one person can express themselves. ·servation, start the sentence with I. Impact, state what the person had ne in a neutral way. Interpretation, say how their action or actions de you feel. Request, as it says, make a request, not an order. It would) help if the company had regular team building activities which build ter relationships within the company. This will definitely lessen the inces of misunderstandings and conflicts popping up. It'll also help luce stress and allow employees to speak up and be heard. Have the) sides engage with each other. You shouldn't lecture the parties; you're tead allowing them a space for their cases to be heard. Each person uld lay bare their grievances against the other party in an vironment that truly feels neutral. One party shouldn't monopolize discussion, nor attempt to undermine the others position. Let one son speak and continue to do so until they finished sharing, then the posing side should stay therapies until they're finished. The objective o find the actual problem, not the faults of the other side. A possible irse of action is to have the meeting with the two opposing parties. en after the discussion has ended, you can leave the room. After the o sides can then talk to one another privately. Here they can work out ir solutions and or just put their hard feelings to rest.

Listen to what your people have to say. Not only should you allow ir staff the space and the time to talk, you should also listen carefully them. If you don't focus on the discussion, they'll think that you n't care for their well-being, especially their emotional well-being in slightest. If what the employees are saying involves a fault of your sition or any other parts of the company, don't get offended, file away information for later and investigated as part of the post conflict)cess. Apply the active listening technique which will greatly help to ire their perspective to the other side. Here's how you go about doing t. Listen well as the person shares their side of the story. Understand at they're trying to say, not just the words they're using. Once an ployee has finished their piece, reiterate what they've told you in a

way that's objective and easy to comprehend. You may ask question:
further clarify the employees point too. You must do this in order
really get to the heart of what they're trying to say. If modifications
needed, restate the situation's details again. Analyze the behavior and :
the personality. Personalities can't be readily controlled, and especi:
not when you're inflamed by a conflict. Sometimes a person doesn't e
realize certain aspects of their personality nor that they come off t
way. If you as a mediator draw attention to it and make that the proble
it'll feel as if you're attacking them personally. Avoiding this is cruc
You can't just tell your employees that they are being condescending
annoying, It's too vague. Look to an employee's behavior instead, p
out an example of a recent incident and address that using object
language. If there have been other instances, you may also bring these
in discussion. However, it's best to have recent examples so the employ
are sure to remember

The road to figuring it all out. Once you've examined the det:
of the situation, you and the opposing parties need to start look
for a root cause. This can be easier said than done. To make it ea:
finding said root cause, you need to keep your parties cooperative e
if they're still on opposing sides. To do this, find things the parties
agree on, such as what they like about the other side. They've got
admit this out loud, even if begrudgingly. They should still be allowed
disagree with things, though it's more controlled. Don't worry so m
that they're disagreeing, disliking or hating something or maybe e
someone. You're building their goodwill using these points of contenti
too. Once you've gotten everyone in a more cooperative mindset, y
are free to analyze where, why and how things went wrong without t
much trouble. Find the highest priority concerns at the moment. I
them into a list if you can. When you're done, summarize everythi
in an easy to grasp manner. After, ask if both sides agree, modify i
you missed something. Work on it all together. The opposing part
are capable of owning up to the problem and solving and given enou

lance. They just need to put their feelings aside and understand one
ther. The opposing parties should do the bulk of the work. You as a
nager or third party are only there to ensure things don't spiral out of
trol. There still may be room for misunderstandings. So, watch out
communication breakdowns at any point during the discussion, as
l as lines of thought that won't result in anything substantial.

There needs to be a civil discussion between the two sides. They're
wed to air grievances but don't let them complain too much. Their
n focus should be to arrive at agreeable solutions after all.
mpromise is key. Each person in the room wants something. These
res may not line up at first glance. Therefore, you must all be prepared
compromise for the sake of finding a solution that's mutually
eficial, and possibly replicable for future situations. During the
:ussion, both sides need to be able to share pressing desires or goals
. why they want them. They should be open and honest about their
:rests. From there, it'll be easier for you the third party to figure out a
ttion that can keep everybody happy. If you understand what makes a
:ain employee tick, you'll be able to more efficiently help them reach
ir goal or goals. Apply this to the conflict resolution process and you'll
:e it in the bag

Planted out, you need to discuss and keep discussing until all the
blems or concerns have been discovered. In order to avoid feeling
rwhelmed, make a list of the complications you found, suss out the
st important ones. You just need to focus on the main problems.
n issue isn't as important, you can always leave it for later or just
get it entirely. It would be marvelous if everything could be talked
and solved in a single day. But things might not be so smooth. The
flict might require more time than what you've set aside for the initial
eting. In that case, best to implement some solutions as soon as the
eting ends in order to take care of a pressing issue. However tentative
plan may involve planning out your next actions. How will they be
le, wants to be done and by when, is it to be done? Having a list

of issues ranging from the most urgent ones to the least, you may t
work on them one by one. Setting up regular meetings to check out I
the employees are doing. And if the solutions are being implemente
initially stated. Out of the box conclusions shouldn't be ruled out. V
an array of employees at work, you may not know who's going to I
heads with whom, until they're already in your office waiting for yo
sort the conflict out. Finding a solution that satisfies everyone invol
can be tricky and require a bit of work, but you need to find it. If
party bows out to the other, it won't be good for the long run. It
be used as ammunition for a future conflict. Don't give in or agre
something too fast. Make sure you come to an appropriate solution
natural way. It's got to feel earned.

Be specific, at the end of the discussion, you've got to make s
everything's crystal clear to everyone in the room. It's your final cha
to make sure that nobody has any qualms or misunderstandings v
written or verbal warning. Lay everything out nice and orderly. Try
to forget any points as your employees might have misunderstandi
later on. As we're the act of listening technique, reiterate every poin
a systematic manner. Ask everyone at the end of your summation, if
missed anything, and if so, restate is needed. Say you're sorry. if yo
a manager, you also need to evaluate yourself. You've got to accept t
part of the issue might involve you, perhaps something you did or di
do. Regardless of the finer details of the situation, neither one sid
the other can be entirely right. And as a leader in the company,
have to take responsibility. Everyone must apologize. Whether your f
was intended or not. Here's how to make a formal apology, realize w
you've done, or what helped the conflict snowball into such a disrup
presence. After you must say to the aggrieved individual, I'm sorr
was wrong, then state why you're wrong. And the reasons why. Tell
other person you want your relationship to go back to the way it v
Ask that person for ways to remedy the solution alongside the soluti
you've already thought up in order to keep the incident from happen

ain. Tell them that you'll take their suggestions to heart, they have be aware that you're making a conscious decision to fix the behavior. k for their forgiveness. Continue working on the conflict for posterity. u can't call the conflict done just because all parties seem satisfied and e meeting was adjourned. Depending on the outcome, you may need have more meetings to discuss the solutions with the same parties perhaps additional or different ones. You need to hold yourself and e company accountable for what happens next. Upon evaluating erything that was divulged in the meeting, you have to document it, en ensure that you're thorough in your investigation.

Here are some possible issues to consider. Was there an issue with mpany processes, equipment or facilities? Are the systems efficient or efficient? Or the staff especially those in positions of power, being ofessional, or the company's policies fair and inclusive to everyone? ave there been any recent changes that the employees are having uble adjusting to or the staff being overwhelmed by their tasks? rhaps they're having trouble with deadlines. Don't forget to knowledge positive change. Observe how the parties you spoke with e doing. See if their behavior has changed for the better and knowledge their progress. Big or small, you must commend your ployees for positive actions. You've got to let your people know that u're invested in their well-being and not just how well they're working your company. Make sure that nobody is struggling with expressing emselves. To stop conflicts before they even occur, your company ould have a culture or environment that allows for feedback or mments. This weeds out potential issues which can cause trouble for e company and its staff. If you don't have such practices in place, then ere's no better time to start than right now. Don't just leave it at setting wn a box for people to write down their comments or criticisms. This ems impersonal, like you won't be that involved in or concerned about ndling the issue. Have one on one meetings with your employees for given amount of time. As for the amount, it depends on how much

time you can spare to talk to everybody. More time will be better. I
15 minutes give or take should be enough to ask someone how they
doing, if there's anything bothering them, if there's something that nee
to be fixed, or if they've got any suggestions. Thinking of the future, if y
want your company to be prosperous, you've got to take on conflicts
the present to pave the way for the future. Resolve conflicts successfu
and you'll reap the benefits. On the other hand, if you put off confli
then you'll ensure that your company is going to be stagnant inefficie
and dreadful to work at. So even as you're in the middle of two host
parties who don't seem like they're cooperating, remember that this is
for the best outcome possible, and a future without much infighting.

And now, it's discussion time. The most important part of t'
training. Whoever's the head honcho in the group should designat
facilitator whose responsibility it is that each of the questions you
on your screen is covered and that everyone time permitting, is able
have their say. Make sure all contributions are valued, all suggestic
considered and all opinions respected.

| Page

Don't miss out!

Visit the website below and you can sign up to receive emails whenev B. Vincent publishes a new book. There's no charge and no obligatio

https://books2read.com/r/B-A-QWUO-RJSPB

BOOKS 2 READ

Connecting independent readers to independent writers.

Also by B. Vincent

Affiliate Marketing
Affiliate Marketing
Affiliate Marketing

Standalone
Affiliate Recruiting
Business Layoffs & Firings
Business and Entrepreneur Guide
Business Remote Workforce
Career Transition
Project Management
Precision Targeting
Professional Development
Strategic Planning
Content Marketing
Imminent List Building
Getting Past GateKeepers
Banner Ads
Bookkeeping
Bridge Pages
Business Acquisition
Business Bogging

Marketing Automation
Better Meetings
Business Conflict Resolution

About the Publisher

cepting manuscripts in the most categories. We love to help people get
:ir words available to the world.

Revival Waves of Glory focus is to provide more options to be
blished. We do traditional paperbacks, hardcovers, audio books and
ooks all over the world. A traditional royalty-based publisher that
:rs self-publishing options, Revival Waves provides a very author
:ndly and transparent publishing process, with President Bill Vincent
olved in the full process of your book. Send us your manuscript and
will contact you as soon as possible.

Contact: Bill Vincent at rwgpublishing@yahoo.com
w.rwgpublishing.com

www.ingramcontent.com/pod-product-compliance
Lightning Source LLC
Chambersburg PA
CBHW030537210326
41597CB00014B/1188